Vivienne Tregenza

Conversations with Magic Stones

Indigo Dreams Publishing

First Edition: Conversations with Magic Stones
First published in Great Britain in 2025 by:
Indigo Dreams Publishing
24, Forest Houses
Cookworthy Moor
Halwill
Beaworthy
Devon
EX21 5UU

www.indigodreamspublishing.com

Vivienne Tregenza has asserted her right under the Copyright, Designs and Patents Act 1988 to be identified as the author of this work.
© Vivienne Tregenza 2025

ISBN 978-1-912876-96-9

British Library Cataloguing in Publication Data. A CIP record for this book can be obtained from the British Library.

This book is sold subject to the condition that it shall not, by way of trade or otherwise, be lent, re-sold, hired out, or otherwise circulated without the author's and publisher's prior consent in any form of binding or cover other than that in which it is published and without a similar condition including this condition being imposed on the subsequent purchaser.

Designed and typeset in Palatino Linotype by Indigo Dreams.
Cover image: Curved Form (Bryher II), 1961 by Barbara Hepworth. Photo credit: San Francisco Museum of Modern Art / Bridgeman Images.
Works and writings by Barbara Hepworth © Bowness.
Printed and bound in Great Britain by 4edge Ltd.

Papers used by Indigo Dreams are recyclable products made from wood grown in sustainable forests following the guidance of the Forest Stewardship Council.

For Colin

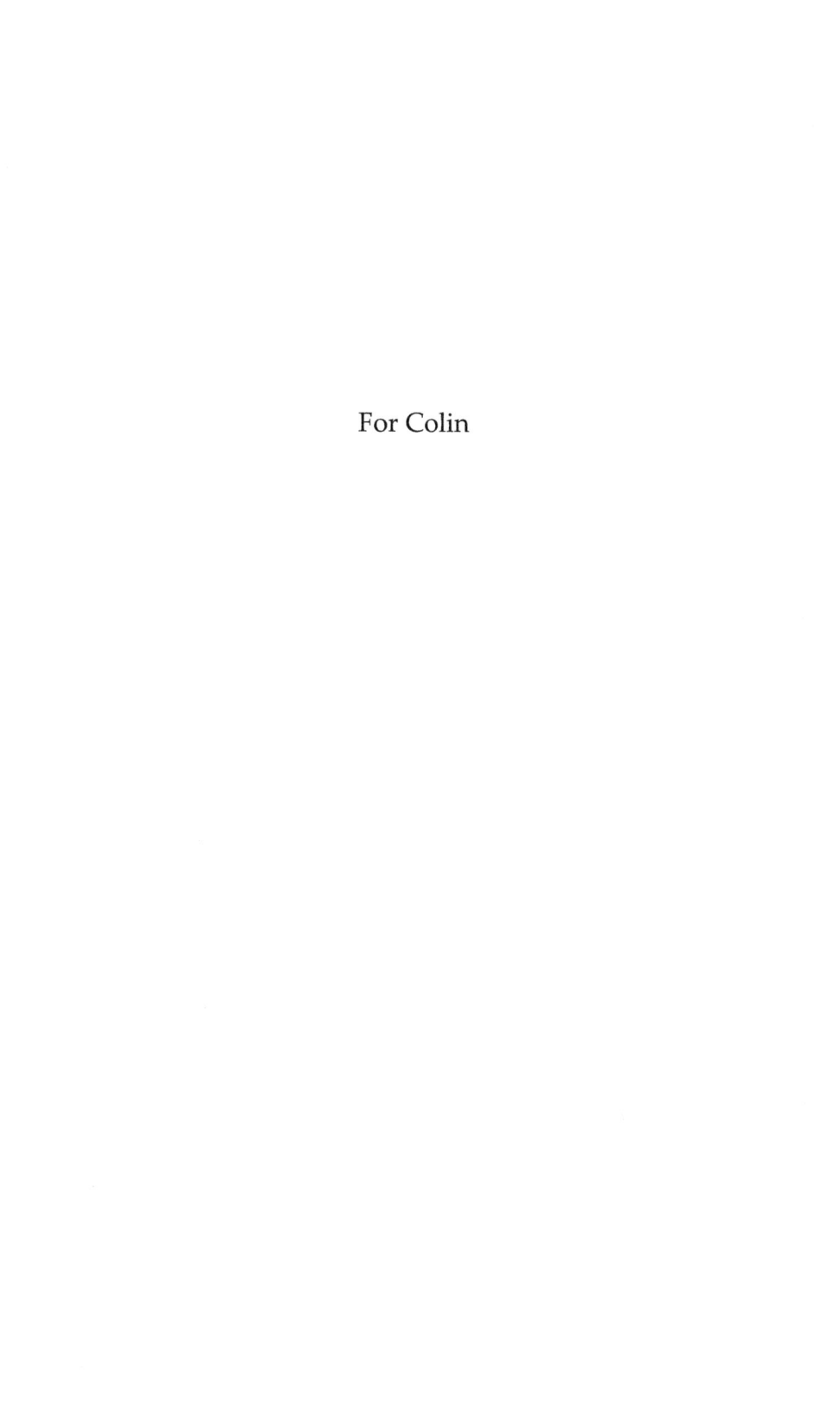

Acknowledgements

Thanks to the editors of the following publications, online magazines and websites in which some of these poems first appeared: *Acumen, ARTEMISpoetry, Did I Tell You? 131 Poems For Children In Need* (WordAid.org.uk), *London Grip, Orbis, Pale Fire: New Writing on the Moon* (The Frogmore Press), *poetry p f, Poetry Salzburg Review, Poetry Scotland, Quintet and other poets* (Cinnamon Press), *Reading Room* (Hermitage Press), *South, The Dawntreader*.

Some of the poems in *Island* were shortlisted in the Cinnamon Press Debut Poetry Prizes 2014, 2016 (runner up) and Poetry Pamphlet Awards 2018, 2023.

An earlier version of 'Midsummer' was in *Light through Stained Glass* longlisted in the Mslexia Poetry Pamphlet Competition 2022.

'Blue' was originally in *Canary in a Glass House* shortlisted for the Cinnamon Press New Voices Award in 2024.

An earlier version of *Form (poems i.m. Barbara Hepworth)* was shortlisted for The Hedgehog Poetry Press 'Proper Poetry Pamphlet Competition' in 2024.

Conversations with Magic Stones was highly commended in the Geoff Stevens Memorial Prize (Indigo Dreams Publishing) 2024.

With love and gratitude to Zeeba Ansari, my first poetry tutor, mentor and friend. Many thanks to Victoria Field, Penelope Shuttle and Angela Stoner for encouragement on workshops in Cornwall in the early days. To Alice Kavounas, appreciation for leading the Poetry School seminars I attended in Penzance in 2012 and 2018.

Warmest thanks to Alex Josephy, my mentor on the Cinnamon Press mentoring scheme, for editorial advice and close reading of this manuscript.

A big thank you to poets Rosie Jackson, Maitreyabandhu and Pippa Little for endorsing this collection. Special thanks to Rosie for her mentoring skills, Maitreyabandhu for helpful suggestions and Pippa for her kindness and enthusiasm.

Many thanks to the Barbara Hepworth Estate for all artistic permissions including the use of a photograph of 'Curved Form (Bryher II), 1961' on the front cover.

My grateful thanks to The Tate, St Ives whose retrospective exhibition of Barbara Hepworth's work in 2023 inspired this project and to the Barbara Hepworth Museum and Sculpture Garden where I spent many happy hours writing some of the poems in this collection.

Sincere gratitude to Dawn Bauling and Ronnie Goodyer for believing in *Conversations with Magic Stones* and for choosing to publish it.

To my friends and family, especially Colin and Lamorna – all my love, always.

Conversations with Magic Stones is Vivienne Tregenza's debut collection.

CONTENTS

Form

Conversations with Magic Stones 13
Pelagos, 1946 14
can you feel me? 15
Balancing Act 16
Held 17
Strung 18
Poised 19
Tides I, 1946 20
Mên-An-Tol 21
Sphere with Inner Form, 1963 22
Madonna and Child, 1954 23
River Form, 1965 24
Come back in the rain 25
Here 26
Tools 27
Pebble 28
Summerhouse Villanelle 29
Taking the Biscuit 30
Two Forms in Echelon, 1961 31
Form 32
There were days 33
One day this summer 34
Sea Form (Porthmeor), 1958 35
Chipping away 36
Thrust 37
Set in Stone 38

Gravyor 39
Passing Through 40
Barbara Hepworth Contemplates the Universe 41
Evening 42

Island

Curved Form (Bryher II), 1961 45
La Coquille 46
Eclipse 47
Island 48
Storm 49
Walled Garden 50
Blessing 51
Anniversary 52
Blue 54
Rain 55
Midsummer 56
Notes on a Butterfly Dream 57
Walled Garden (ii) 58
Eden Rock 59
Pelagos, 2023 60
Mên-An-Tol (ii) 61
Song for Lamorna 62
Letter to C 63

NOTES 64

Conversations with Magic Stones

Form

Poems i.m. Barbara Hepworth (1903-1975)

'And the poem, I think, is only
your voice speaking'

~ Virginia Woolf, *The Waves*

Conversations with Magic Stones

I heard the rhythm of the sculptor's hammer
through the sea-walls of the womb;
cradled in the hollow of her coombe,
I felt the contours of my mother.

I grew to love other shapes and structures,
their textures, concavities; holding
conversations with magic stones, nurturing
a passion for the mysteries of sculpture.

In my adopted home, working through the night,
I sought a *perfect equilibrium*; expression
of a true idea relating to creation.
Thrust and rise of forms. Shadows cast by light.

Sculptor poised between coast and moor,
I heard wind mould granite, waves carve the shore.

Pelagos, 1946

I see the sculptor
at the centre
of this bright necklace
of houses strung along the bay,
held in its curve
looking out towards the sea
and distant shorelines.

I imagine her
finishing her morning coffee,
lighting a cigarette or two,
eager to get on
with the day's work,
to feel the warmth
of wood beneath her hands.

The light is Mediterranean
as she carves
to the rhythm
of a hammering heartbeat,
counterpoint
to the screams
of wind and water.

can you feel me?

> *I am the hollow*
> fill me with cave-water, blue
> echoes of the sea

I am …the contour
the gently curving breast
   of Yorkshire hills

> *I …am the landscape*
> of valley and village, I am
> every rise and fall

I am…the thrust
I will push through darkness
   to emerge, sunlit

> *I am the form*
> reflected in these works,
> can you feel me?

Balancing Act

Shaped by two counties,
touched by two lovers,
four children tugging
at her heartstrings,
the sculptor juggled
many lives.

Stretched by the demands
of motherhood and art,
villager and worldly star,
she performed
a balancing act:

feeling the tension
between land and sea,
caught in the undertow
but never drowning,
rising always to stand
on solid ground.

Held

Each one of us a shape
    contained in structures,
every memory unique
in its angles and dimensions –
the brick trolleys we squeezed into
to hurtle down the garden path,
the gazebo at Tregeseal; hexagonal walls
enclosing the rough floor we lay on,
    those cracked wooden steps
in the old barn

each long rectangle
    precarious beneath our feet.

Strung

too taut, I snapped –
broken string
no music in me

Restrung
over the hollow
of my fractured form

I became
a plucked string
that keeps on ringing

Poised

on the edge, I find
my balance again

here on the cliff
of this sculpture garden

where voids are full
of air and colour

and nothing gives way
to everything.

Here, space is made new
and all our ideas

of what is palpable, real,
are turned upside-down.

Hepworth's gift to us. How
to journey through chaos

to find a centre. How
to make the centre hold.

Tides I, 1946

From a solid trunk
another form emerges –
scoured curve of rock,

contours of a seascape –
the rolling waves heard
on the pebbled beach

and the peepholes made
to see through something solid
to what lies beyond –

that blue-green world
of ocean or headland
which draws us in

to see with fresh eyes
what we knew was there.

Mên-An-Tol

Not far from Trewyn
there's another holed stone –

Crick Stone to mend a crooked back,
cure for rickets and childish ills,

Devil's Eye for a changeling,
fertility ring, site of longing

for a child, where I was reborn
among the furze and heather

one Spring morning, three years
to the day I gave birth at last.

The air was still and fertile as
this Hepworth garden –

everything nurtured
with a mother's care.

Sphere with Inner Form, 1963

Here's my element, my sphere,
my world within a world

and here's my voice, imagined, heard
above the birdsong of the garden

telling my assistants to place the sculpture
here, beside the roundness

of the flowering quince so other mothers
in the future see the light

glance off its surface, recognise
these shapes and feel their wholeness.

We rear our offspring to soar
like gulls above the harbour

for mothers can't keep their children safe.
But I won't forget the way

my body curved around you,
held you, lulled in water for a while.

Madonna and Child, 1954
(i.m Paul Skeaping)

Light falls
   on a mother's grieving form
and on the face
   of her baby, hoisted
forever on her hip, his small hand
   clutching her heart
as he reaches for a last kiss

a moment chiselled in shadow,
   held in stone.

River Form, 1965

The sculptor made a river
of her joy and grief.
She carved a cave of water

with apertures revealing colour;
three portals looking out to leaf
and flower, banks of the river

on either side. This sculpture
coraled like a living reef
has gathered rain water,

liquid sunshine flows like amber
into a green womb beneath
the belly of the river.

If she were here, the sculptor,
would she confirm my own belief;
though caves may fill with water –

for all emotions matter
in this life which is so brief –
yet light can reach the river
as the river swells with water?

Come back in the rain

and see how all your work
has weathered the wind-scoured years,

return and hear the drumming knuckles
of rainfall on the greenhouse roof,

step back inside and feel your sculptures
recalling all the lives you lived,

take up your tools, cobwebbed
and rusting here, begin again

to carve your unique forms.
The garden's missing you,

the seat beside the summerhouse
sits empty now.

Here

are the chisels, the hammers, the tools;
here are the rasps she always used.

Here are the aprons that she wore.
Here are the dents in the studio floor.

Here are the marble cubes she touched;
here are the views she loved so much.

Here are her trees, her shrubs, her flowers.
Here are her summers, her striking hours.

Here is her light and here her dark;
here is the place she left her mark.

Tools

The poet is a sculptor
setting out her tools –
white rectangles,
tiny sharp chisels
of pencil and pen,
her *thinking hand* clutching
the table as the writing hand
finds its form
through the scattered thoughts,
disparate notes, blotches
and crossings out
to something familiar
     and strange.

Pebble

This is the way to chisel a poem –
    chipping at language
hammering out the form
    looking for new angles
and smoothing its edges.

Or sometimes without any effort
    a poem is found
moulded and scoured –
    small pebble balancing
on the broken shoreline.

Summerhouse Villanelle

The summerhouse is painted white;
white the walls, the bed, the door
and all reflect the shimmering light

that glances off the sculptures, bright
monuments to all that went before.
This garden flowers bronze and white

in rhyme with every sculpted form; sight
viewed by thousands, thousands more
drawn to these harmonies, this light.

Did she nap here each afternoon, might
this be her place to dream and draw?
What could she see through the white

windows of this small room? A flight
of birds, shadows of a tree? What she saw
remains a mystery infused with light

but what she left behind is her delight
in rhythm, structure and in form.
The summerhouse is painted white.
It shimmers in the morning light.

Taking the Biscuit

Would Dame Barbara have wished
to be remembered as an icon?
Maybe. But it's her humanness
that makes her real. Her imperfection.

Take this. A funny story told
of her assistants in the greenhouse, sworn
to secrecy, out of sight as she entertained
potential buyers on the lawn…

One student, a certain Terry Frost,
caught short, released a golden stream
into a flower pot. It slowly dribbled down
the garden path and on and on between

the legs of those important folk.
That week he didn't get a chocolate
biscuit with his tea! He passed the story on
for every stone has magic in it.

Two Forms in Echelon, 1961

One person leans
towards another. Can you hear
their conversation?

Are these military orders
from superior to lower rank?
Are these the whisperings

of war or some nonsense
heard in the village, passed on
by word of mouth –

bits of gossip, noisy
as seagulls –
by a meddlesome chorus

of players, each rehearsed
in their parts, keeping their ears
to the ground for news

of *emmets* or incomers
from up north with *their strange
ways and goings-on*?

Form

Each piece had its form
different to any other;
structure and rhythm the norm
for this sculptor, lover, mother

different to any other.
She forged a new direction.
Sculptor, lover, mother –
always feeling the tension

as she forged a new direction
in the trajectory of her art,
always feeling the tension…
Alongside. Together. Apart.

In the trajectory of her art
she felt herself complete
alongside, together or apart,
in shadow and in light.

She felt herself complete;
structure and rhythm her norm
in shadow and in light
as she worked to find her form.

There were days

    when sea mist rolled in,
covering boats in the harbour
with a white cloud you could taste.

A salt that covered the houses.
Downalong a giant shroud –
ghostly, still. You could be anywhere

and nowhere. Sculptures
in the Hepworth garden
disappeared in the milky soup.

Those were days
when the path to the studio
was slippery beneath her feet

and she felt her way
like a blind woman. Outside
every sound muffled –

inside, silence broken
by the rhythmic beat
of a ringing hammer

as she held onto what guided her –
as she laid hands
on the one constant thing.

One day this summer

I hear a voice *Rise from your sick bed
and follow this golden thread…*

Down the dreary street to the station,
two short train rides and I'm here again

dipping my burning feet in the waves,
walking on shimmering sands.

Above the beach, artists are painting
or eating or making love.

Church bells measure the passing hours.
The sun hammers down on a labyrinth

of alleyways. I catch the golden thread
that leads to a garden high on a hill.

Could heaven be here
on a day like this, the light of paradise

glancing off these forms, leading us
back to ourselves?

Sea Form (Porthmeor), 1958

I watch this dancing wave
transfigured into solid form

a rockface cracked and slippery –
and suddenly I'm back with you

on a Cornish beach
where you fall and bang your head.

The next day I won't leave you.
We lie beached on the double bed

where I nurse you with a wet flannel,
there there of my nine-year old self

as the family leave for the coast.
But you're already leaving,

my name down for boarding school
from where you'll drive away, mum

at the end of summer –
the end of all my summers –

the sky split open
like a head wound

as my legs give way.

Chipping away

…this doubt that I can do her justice – she, a sculptor with my mother's eyes who leads me through the streets of her adopted home to this garden full of light, graced with all she left behind.

Just reflect she whispers, *all you need is here.*

I'll leave the details and opinions to historians, biographers, as I return again
        to what still stands –

A single form thrust upwards to the morning light that dazzles us with brightness.

Two forms that lean towards each other as dusk brings to the garden a secret dark.

A form within a form that breaks my heart.

Part of the conversation, I'll leave my small marks here:

imperfectly

        insistently

                chipping away

Thrust
(found historical definitions)

1510 **act of pressing**

What is this pressure on her materials Hepworth brought to bear? Was it a kind of love?

1580 **act of thrusting**

To make something *that will win*. Always a rising up from the darkness towards light.

1708 **propulsive force**

Pure energy – like something launched into space.

1968 **principal theme**

The thrust of Hepworth's ideas: to find the *poetic structure* in everything.

Set in Stone

Here on a granite rock,
waves swirling around my feet,
I wonder how it came to be

that molten lava cooled
in the burning belly of the earth
to give us quartz,

feldspar, mica; how it thrust
through the fragile ground
two hundred million years ago.

I think of the long wearing
of water. How many years
it takes the sea to scour

something solid into sand
that glitters underfoot.
I watch a child knock her castle

down and start again. In the end
everything's washed away,
even sculptures carry cracks

that deepen as time passes.
So does it matter if our words
are set in stone, or not?

Gravyor

O Gravyor, with blazing hands chiselling
through the pain, lost in the creation
of new miracles of stone, you're carving

out your place in future landscapes, leaving
sculpted legacies; true expressions
of a Gravyor with gifted hands. Chiselling

rock until a form takes shape, sculpting
ovals, spheres, arcs with a passion
for the miracle of stone. Carving

contours of the land, you find meaning
in materials, in granite conversations.
Gravyor, with hands worn from chiselling

(light on your moving figure creating
shadows on emerging forms), attention
to the miracle of stone sees you carving

its endless possibilities, glittering
dimensions. You feel secrets in its tensions.
O Gravyor, graced with hands for chiselling
miraculous stone carvings.

Passing Through

Our Gravyor is here
    in the gull-crazy streets
        of this old seaside town,

remembered in the church
    and in the winding alleys
        where I'm walking down

towards the beach
    where ropes of boats are
        strung at angles, slack or taut.

She's here, and there
    a few miles away
        on the blustery moors

where a piper plays a tune
    rising from the sacred land
        on this Penwith afternoon,

of course she's here too
    granite-strong, wind-strung
        and like us, passing through.

Barbara Hepworth Contemplates the Universe

Did the spheres sing for her
on Goonhilly Downs
and was she captured
by alien circles, lifting
their shiny faces
towards the sun and moon?

Were her thoughts filled
with galaxies –
clusters of stars –
as she travelled back
to the heart
of her adopted home?

Everything precious held
in the curve of the bay,
her thoughts stitching
the evening sky like swallows –
their shape shifting
twists and turns –

the circles of her mind
reflecting the great circles
of the universe; mystery
of beginnings and endings
how they meet
at the same place

to make matter
or a perfect void
through which we're born
into this world from where
at last we step out, dazzled
into the dark.

Evening

I see Hepworth in her garden at the end
of the day, a cigarette between her lips,
she's coughing a little (a burning at the back
of her throat) so she takes a sip of whisky.
Her voice is husky as she discusses with
her assistants where to place her latest work.

All that matters is how it will stand in relation
to the trees and shrubs. How the light
will strike it. Where the shadows will fall.
She's tired. A decade of cancer treatment
and international travel. Time now
to sit inside the summerhouse and rest.

She looks so small beside these towering
shapes. I wonder if she knows it will be her last
evening, this cigarette her last but one.
Did she glimpse something shining through
the clouds or was this just another day
in her studio, feeling her way forward?

Island

'Perhaps what one wants to say
is formed in childhood…'

~ Barbara Hepworth

Curved Form (Bryher II), 1961

We rowed across the water
in your red rowing boat –

you with your cricket cap on,
cricket jersey draped over your shoulders

a big grin on your face as we shared
this secret between us.

She was only eight weeks –
small as a sea anemone and clinging

to my sea-wall. I remember
the red-gold of the bracken

as we walked around the island,
the September sun on our backs.

Do you recall the rocks
on the beach scoured smooth

by the wind which sang like sea-strings
through the cracks?

How we leant against them.
How you laid your hands on my belly.

That day we believed in miracles.

La Coquille
Mais je t'aime comme le coquillage aime son sable (B. Péret)

You promised to keep me
    safe above the tide
as we lay in a sandy hollow;
      this new thing between us
        held as gently
as a rare shell you'd found

on Pentle Bay.
I dreamt that we were wading
    in the shallows
as swimmers rose from the sea
saying *Go deeper,*
it's beautiful out there

Did I really feel
    your soul like water
gliding next to mine
    as a purple heron
took flight
    from the Great Pool?

How did we find each other
    at last
    on the crumbling shoreline
of this island, alive
with the sound of terns
    and oystercatchers?

Eclipse
Tresco, Isles of Scilly (11.08.1999)

The way you came to me
on Appletree Carn, silhouetted, balancing
bubbly, two fluted glasses…
What else? Oh yes! The way the birds flew
through the darkening sky. The way the cows
lay down – warm boulders in the field below,
a coral band of light on the horizon and
the way your arms encircled mine. Such warmth!

We watched the sun embrace
the moon over Saffron Cove,
a moment only.
For us – a lifetime.
Two worlds turned upside down!
Everything new and ringed with gold.

Island

Stumbling over gorse and heather
on the criss-crossed paths

we brace ourselves
against the wind

You're mouthing something
impossible to hear

as you take my hand
and lead me down

from the castle on the moor
to shelter at Old Grimsby

As the years pass and you struggle
again with words

I'll find you there

Storm
(after *Stone Form (Tresco)* by Barbara Hepworth)

The wind was screeching
in the Monterey pines

and a flock of turnstones
suddenly erupted

from one of the trees –
chattering explosion of feathers –

as the weather drenched
my summer clothes, black clouds

glowering above me.
I was walking towards you

walking for the sake
of walking in the rain

washed clean of words
as I stumbled towards home –

small bothy on an island
and you, my love, inside.

Walled Garden
(Tresco, Isles of Scilly)

That first evening in the Abbey
we look at a shady courtyard
next to The Old Servants' Hall.

How can the two of us
imagine a garden there?

Preferring to spend
those summer evenings
on the edges of the island

beyond the *amaryllis belladonna,
banskia* and bottlebrushes,

we grow food for our table;
beetroot and broad beans,
Sun Gold, Bright Lights, Rainbow Chard

iron and folic acid
for the growing child.

Blessing

You came to us on a shooting star
little creature from outer space,
unformed moon-walker.
Spotted on the radar, we knew at once you were ours
(although I had to wait an age to hold you,
me with my swelling belly, my sea legs).
Then one day, there you were with your open-mouthed cry,
your newly-wrinkled hands,
blue eyes blinking hard in the bright glare.
You nuzzled, kid-like, butting your mother,
drank your fill, sweet guzzler
until you slept, replete.
We watched your tiny form in awe.
A blessing, blessed, complete.

Anniversary

We cross water to reach
our anniversary celebration
at the Roseland Hotel

where we arrive, a family of three:
she in her contented curve of sleep,
the two of us – deep in conversation.

As we walk along the nearby beach
she shoots ahead – hooded shrimp
jumping on the coiled

casts of lugworms,
hearing the sea breathe in her ear –
our gooseberry sea squirt.

Below our feet, heart urchins stir
in the shifting sand
as a sudden slab of rock takes me

back: *Flung towels, costumes drying,*
packed lunches in uniform paper bags.
A hidden hunger. An ache in the seascape.

Above us, the afternoon light pales, becomes
a white sheet tucked tight at the corners
on the sky's empty bed.

That night, we can't leave our child
with strangers so take her to eat with us
in her high chair, stared at by elderly folk

used to leaving children elsewhere.
Later, sleepless, I open the window
to taste a salty dark

vast as the ocean
of memory ebbing and flowing.
Invisible tides.

Blue

There in the top drawer
between a lock of hair
and a silver charm

a strip of white
with two lines
running through

I had another
somewhere
just the same

pale as the first
snowdrop rising
from the black earth

twice crossed with blue
colour of the aching sky

Rain

rose petals delicate rain
Words on the fridge door
of our first home

On our wedding day

I threw *rose petals* in your hair
which you shook
to make me laugh

We laughed a lot that day

Then came the *delicate rain*
our ark dipping under a wave
as you tried to keep us steady

Me bailing out like crazy

Now the rain has seeped
into the earth and the *rose
petals* are dry – potpourri

Midsummer

Ahead of us, Lamorna runs
with River, the dog's tail
in tune with the quaking grass
while I trace moving patterns
of sunlight on your face,
heat rising from the lit path
as sea-barley leaves
rough kisses on our legs.

Beyond the cliff-edge
glittering water, broken
here and there
by a dark boulder.
Above us, a soft white line
on the sky's cornflower blue –
a feather left floating
when another child fell?

We can't be sure.
No, we can't be sure of anything
on this longest day
but laughter rising
from a hidden cove
where our daughter delights
to find her spaniel
swimming in the waves.

Notes on a Butterfly Dream

Safe as a ship in a bottle,
we're part of the landscape
in this house of windows, watching

the cartwheeling clouds, hearing
the creaking trees, gazing through glass
at swaying green; blue hills
basking in sunshine.

Gone are the college rooms, dismal bedsits.
Here light pours into every space
and we're looking across the fields

towards our daughter's one-room school
where she settles like that butterfly
she's captured on scrap paper; transforming
everything she touches.

Walled Garden (ii)

It took us time
    to grow a garden here
in this seaside town
    with the sound of gulls
circling overhead.

Here's *aeonium purpureum*
    each Scilly cabbage
a memory sculpted
    from the crevices
of dry stone walls

and here's *geranium maderense*
    thriving still, surviving
the March frost that killed
    all growth
that dreadful Spring.

Next year I'll plant
    nerine bowdenii and to this
rosy canvas I'll add
    agapanthus just a touch
of blue.

Eden Rock
(for Lamorna Beth)

She's first, the only one
who's never climbed before, not fluent
in the language of the climb, stumbling

over words she needs to understand
ascent. What still voice whispers
Choose this handhold, place your foot here

as the cliff rises sheer above her?
The sun glints off the rock face like a knife's edge.
Unfazed, she changes feet, grips hard

with two small hands. Below,
the man with the belay rope
looks calmly on; it creaks and slips in the piton

as she steps up and up towards the top,
turns to wave then leans away from safety,
bracing steady feet against the cliff. Anchored

to the rock face, she abseils down to meet us.
Mum, Dad, that was so cool!
You looked so small!

How will we, left holding clothes
she'll soon outgrow, adjust our step
to this new child?

Pelagos, 2023
(St Ives)

We're held by this bay –
headlands like huge arms
on either side
and we're looking out
to the incoming tide's
white lacework of waves,
surfers like basking lizards
in the distance…
This could be Greece you say.

But this is our land,
warm-brown with bracken,
dotted with yellow
scribbles of gorse
and we're looking out
towards turquoise,
the hard years behind us,
embracing whatever lies
beyond The Island.

Mên-An-Tol (ii)

Grateful for this purple heather,
honey scented gorse, growing
where we picked sprigs
for our wedding table
seventeen summers ago.

With us, our grown up daughter
scanning the landscape…
Beside her, our elderly spaniel
unsteady on the path to Mên-An-Tol.
Beyond the boggy terrain

Ding Dong mine in the distance
and above our heads
geese writing a letter in the sky
as they fly above Mounts Bay,
their shapes backlit

by golden light. Our hearts
still beat to the rhythm
of those white wings –
each day we're breaking
into song and taking flight.

Song for Lamorna

Mounts Bay lies beaten,
burnished as Newlyn Copper,

the shoreline scattered
with the debris of our lives.

We trip from time to time
as we look to the horizon.

When the light fades we retreat
to a balcony above the beach.

It's warm for September.
You've got your father's eyes.

               We're here
beneath skies turning

to a shade of Cornish Slate; the bay
strung with coloured gems.

Letter to C

On the horizon –
the delicate calligraphy
of distant islands

where our first notes
were written, love letters
winging across the waters.

We're writing our lives –
St Mary's just a smudge today
on a clear blue line,

our book of words
full of blotches
and crossings-out

worn at the edges,
the paper thumbed and crusted,
the script shaky

but still our morning pages
fill with the sound of seagulls
and the break of day.

NOTES

Mên-an-Tol (p. 21) meaning *holed stone* in Cornish, is part of a Bronze Age stone monument near Madron in West Cornwall. The hole in the stone is just big enough for people to squeeze through; in local folklore it has been linked to fertility and even as a cure for rickets.

Taking the Biscuit (p. 30): Thanks to Anthony Frost for this anecdote about his father the artist Sir Terry Frost (1915-2003).

Two Forms in Echelon, 1961 (p. 31): *emmets* is a word used by the Cornish to describe visitors to Cornwall. Derived from an old dialect word meaning 'ants', it supposedly sees similarities as they arrive in the summer and swarm around!

There were days (p. 33): *Downalong* is the name traditionally given to the area near the harbour of narrow streets, lanes and courtyards that used to house the fishing community of St Ives.

Gravyor (p. 39): In 1968 Dame Barbara Hepworth was invited to become a Bard of *Gorsedh Kernow*, the body that celebrates and promotes Cornwall's Celtic culture and heritage. She took the Cornish name *Gravyor* as her bardic title, meaning *Sculptor*.

Barbara Hepworth Contemplates the Universe (p. 41): Goonhilly Earth Station is located on the Lizard Peninsular. In 1962 Hepworth was invited to visit the satellite station which made a big impression on her and influenced her work.

Song for Lamorna (p. 62): Newlyn Copper dates from 1890 when Newlyn artist, John Drew MacKenzie, set up the *Newlyn Industrial Class*, a specialised arts and crafts training facility. In the winter, fishermen were taught metalworking techniques like *repousée*, where copper sheets would be hammered or beaten into such items as plates, vases, jugs and trays with elaborate designs.